# ELGIN CATHEDRAL

## The Cathedral Kirk of Moray

History by H. B. MACKINTOSH

Description by J. S. RICHARDSON

GW00675674

EDINBURGH

HER MAJESTY'S STATIONERY OFFICE

ISBN 0 11 491604 7

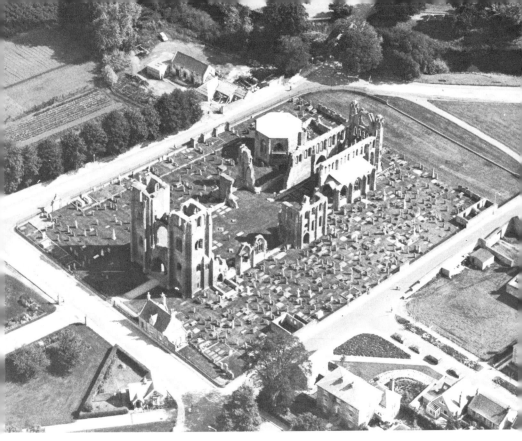

Plate 1.  Aerial photograph from the south-west. Compare block plan below and notes opposite.

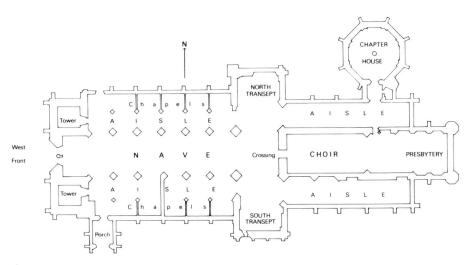

ELGIN CATHEDRAL stands on the southern side of the river Lossie, outside the ancient boundaries of the burgh of Elgin. The Cathedral of Moray developed through much of the thirteenth century, from the removal of the seat of the diocese from Spynie (where the Bishop's Palace remained) to Elgin in 1224. 'The ornament of the realm, the glory of the kingdom, the delight of foreigners and stranger guests', the church was one of the largest in the kingdom, being exceeded in length only by St Andrews Cathedral. Major repair was needed after the cathedral was burned in 1390 by Alexander Stewart Earl of Buchan, the 'Wolf of Badenoch'. The central tower was subsequently reconstructed by Bishops Innes and Henry de Lychton, but part of it fell again in 1506 and its repair was perhaps the last major work undertaken before the Reformation.

Then deprived of its functions and its revenues, the cathedral fell into decay, aided by the stripping of lead from its roofs in 1567. The central tower collapsed in 1711; the shell was used as a quarry for building material, reducing the fabric during the eighteenth century to much the same appearance as it has today. The chapter-house alone remained fairly intact, for it still had a function as a meeting place for the Incorporated Trades until 1731.

As a consequence of the annexation of the property of the bishop-rics, the Crown had a better claim than anyone else to ownership of the cathedral, and the Barons of the Exchequer (then the Scottish name for the Treasury) were first persuaded to concern themselves with repair in the early nineteenth century. Successive government departments accepted the duty of maintenance, and today this outstanding medieval building is cared for as an ancient monument by the Secretary of State for Scotland.

The description on the following pages begins at the WEST FRONT and proceeds through the cathedral from west to east (air photograph and block plan opposite):

The NAVE, the part of the building open to the laity, flanked on each side by two AISLES, the outer aisles subdivided as a row of CHAPELS;

The CROSSING (from which rose the mid-tower) at the junction of the main body of the cathedral and the TRANSEPTS, which project at right angles to each side;

The CHOIR, enclosed by walls and containing the stalls of the clergy and choristers who performed the daily round of services, and leading on to

The PRESBYTERY to the east of the choir, which housed the high altar and the ceremonial area around it;

AISLES extend to each side of the eastern arm, with a chapel at the end of each;

The CHAPTER-HOUSE, the place of an assembly for the dean, office-bearers and canons of the cathedral to discuss business.

Plate 2. The west front: from R. W. Billings, *The Baronial and Ecclesiastical Antiquities of Scotland* (Edinburgh 1845–52).

# DESCRIPTION

## West Front

The west front of the Cathedral with its flanking towers is suggestive of French influence. The towers with their elongated buttresses are in the First Pointed style; each was 27.4 m (90 ft) high, contained four storeys and terminated in a lead-covered wooden spire. Access to the first floors is by a wheel-stair at the south-east angle of the southern tower. The entrance to the stairway at ground level was originally on the outside of the Kirk and faced eastwards. At first it was intended to carry this stairway up higher but, an alteration being made in the plan, it was ceiled with a rib-and-panel vault at the first-floor level. This vault is of star formation ornamented with carved keystones or bosses at the junction of the ribs. The ascent to the upper floors and the tower-heads was by wheel-stairs in the walls at the abutments of the intervening gable. These stairs are entered from the ends of the arcaded gallery connecting the towers at the first-floor level, and were also connected by passages at the sill level of the great window and at the wall-walk level above it. There was access from these stairways to the clerestory passages and the wall-walks of the nave. The interior walls of the tower still show the effect of the heat caused by the burning timbers of the floors and the spires. In the reconstruction of the northern tower a vaulted ceiling and new windows were introduced into the first-floor chamber. This room now contains many fragments of carved and moulded details.

The great west door (Plate 3) is crowned by triple, crocketted gablets, each of which contains an arcaded panel, enriched with typical thirteenth-century dog-tooth and trefoil patterns. The central gablet has a string course ornamented with dragonesque carvings and the panels of the side gablets are flanked by quatrefoils. The recessed ingo of the doorway is in the First Pointed style; it consists of eight engaged shafts with round-moulded caps and bases with a simple cavetto between each shaft. The arch contains amongst the boldly cut mouldings four rows of dog-tooth, two of stem and trefoil, and an outer order which had a vine-and-leaf decoration; all these enrichments were undercut. The inner screen of the portal with the two doorways is a reconstruction after the 1390 burning and is in the Second Pointed style. The carvings are typical of the period.

Bands of realistic oak branches with leaf and acorn and vine leaf and stem outline the doorways. Above the doorways is a vesica-shaped panel framed with a 'vine' enrichment and furnished at its base with a corbel in leaf form. This panel formerly contained a carved representation of the Holy Trinity to whom the Cathedral Kirk was dedicated. On either side of the panel are kneeling angels with swinging censers surrounded by sprays of leaves.

The great window, occupying the wall space above the portal, is also a reconstruction after 1390. The original gable with its group of lancets was destroyed by the intense heat of the conflagration which had raged furiously at this end of the Kirk. When the present window was complete with tracery it presented a design of considerable elegance, the upper part containing a highly developed 'wheel' pattern and the lower an arrangement of seven lights. It will be noticed that it is not centred between the two towers. A possible explanation for this is that the window was drawn out to full size and prepared at the quarry and that a mistake was made in the dimensions. The wall-walk passing above the window was furnished with a traceried parapet behind which rose the apex of the gable. The parapet was carried by the existing corbel-course. It is enriched with oak-leaf design and has as a central feature the royal arms of Scotland—a shield charged with a lion rampant within a double tressure flory counterflory, suspended by a guige from an oak branch. Flanking this shield on the dexter side, at a slightly lower level, is a shield similarly hung, charged with three cushions lozengeways, within a royal tressure, for the See of Moray. On the sinister side is a shield with guige attached and supported by a pastoral staff. The shield bears a lion rampant within a bordure charged with eight roses, the arms of Bishop Columba de Dunbar (1422–1436), the builder of the reconstructed gable.

## Nave

On entering the Cathedral (Plate 4) it will be noticed that the lower part of the internal façade of the gable has been refaced when the doorway was reconstructed and that the arcaded mural passage is also a work of the early fifteenth-century period but carried out in the older style of architecture. Human faces, leaf patterns and owls are represented in the carved corbels of the hood mouldings of the arcading and on the sides of the towers, which face each other. The stone benches, the corbels, the arches and the upper wall surfaces, as well as the responds at the angles of the towers, are all repair work. This part of the building still bears evidence of the 1390 burning, especially where the masonry above the wall-benching on the south side of the northern tower is split and discoloured.

The nave arcade, which is now reduced to ground level, had six 'bays' or divisions, each being marked on the exterior elevations by buttresses. The full height of the Cathedral Kirk and the outline of its steep-pitched roof can be judged by the west gable. The clerestory windows (those above the level of the aisle roofs) were connected by a mural passage which led round the building and gave access for the

Plate 4.   Inside the nave: the internal face of the west wall.

Plate 5.   The cathedral from the north in the late seventeenth century. The mid-tower is still standing with the great figures of Bishop Innes and a knight in position.
From J. Slezer, *Theatrum Scotiae* (1693).

care and maintenance of the glass. The broken ends of these passages can be seen where they emerge from the western towers. Above them are the entrances from the towers to the wall-walks of the nave.

Unlike contemporary buildings in England, this Scottish cathedral never had a triforium or blind storey; this was due to the unusual height of the nave arcading and to the flat pitch of the timber roofs of the original aisles. The porch was an important feature of the south façade; it was ceiled with rib-and-panel vaulting and furnished with an upper storey. There is no evidence to show that a porch was built for the corresponding doorway in the north aisle.

It has already been indicated that the oldest part of the south aisle extension is in the three easternmost bays. They were unlike the other aisles in that they were ceiled with timber and not with stone. The carved caps of the responds and wall corbels show variations of the 'water leaf' motif; wyverns are introduced into one of these patterns. An interesting and unusual feature in the architecture of this aisle is the interlacing of the arch mouldings, which suggests foreign influence. The aisle appears to have been built during the third quarter of the thirteenth century. The treatment of the nave exterior elevations was unique in Britain, each 'bay' having a separate gable roof which, instead of running into the main wall of the nave, was hipped, thus keeping the lighting of the clerestory windows free from obstruction. The traceried windows in the second and third bays of the south aisle are reconstructions of fifteenth-century date. Each division of the outer aisles provided a chapel dedicated to a particular saint or saints. These chapels were partitioned off by parclose screens of oak and were furnished with wall-presses or aumbries and with piscinae. At the east end of the nave was the fifteenth-century rood-screen and loft.

## Crossing

Above the crossing rose the mid-tower with its great supporting pillars (Plate 5). It was rebuilt during the episcopates of Bishop Innes (1407–1414) and Bishop Henry de Lychton (1414–1422) but in 1506, during the episcopate of Andrew Forman, part of it fell and its restoration begun in the following year was not completed until thirty years later. The tower may have had a lantern lighted by an arched window in the centre of each wall, with an internal arcade above the level of the arches and ceiled with a fine rib-and-panel vault. Fragments of carved ornament, which apparently belonged to this part of the tower, are worthy subjects for the study of design and workmanship. The examples to be noted are the leaf-and-berry enriched caps of the great pillars, the caps from the smaller pillars of the internal arcading, and the animal and heraldic bosses from the ceiling which are now in the collection of architectural carvings preserved in the chambers of the western tower.

The mid-tower was higher than the western towers. A stairway in the north-west angle led to the tower-head which was furnished with a parapet and spire, replaced later by a gabled roof similar to that on the mid-tower of the neighbouring Priory Kirk of Pluscarden.

In the south aisle are set up the remains of the two large-scale figures from the tower; one represents Bishop Innes and the other a knight. These statues once stood in leaf-enriched corbelled niches at the exterior angles on the west side of the tower. The Bishop (Plate 6) is coped and mitred and holds the pastoral staff in his gloved left hand, his right hand having been raised in benediction. The remains of the other figure display the military costume of the early fifteenth century, i.e., tippet of chain mail, armpieces of plate, a short surcoat girded with a massive and ornamented sword-belt, a long shirt of chain mail with thigh-pieces of plate and armour for the lower part of the legs; the left hand grasps a dagger and the right has held a sword pointing downwards.

Bishop Innes was buried beside the north-west pillar of the crossing. The monument, of which a few fragments remain, was of considerable size and displayed a life-size kneeling figure of the Bishop, placed on the top of the tomb-chest and under a richly moulded canopy with 'saints' and 'angels' and vine and oak motifs. The effigy, now headless, was recovered from the fallen debris of the tower and it occupies a temporary stance at the east end of the south aisle of the nave. Vested in alb and cope, the figure is kneeling on a cushion which lies on a stool covered with linen-fold drapery. The gloved hands are joined in an attitude of prayer and the pastoral staff is supported against the left shoulder. The tomb-chest on which the figure was mounted bore an inscription in two lines and of this there is now only a detached fragment. It reads:

*per septennium potenter edificavit et*
*diligenter continuavit et obiit anno dmni*

. . . for seven years he built vigorously and
diligently continued, and died in the year . . .

A record dating from the close of the seventeenth century gives the whole of the missing portion, except the date, as

Here lies the Reverend Father in Christ John Innes,
bishop of this church, who began this outstanding work . . .

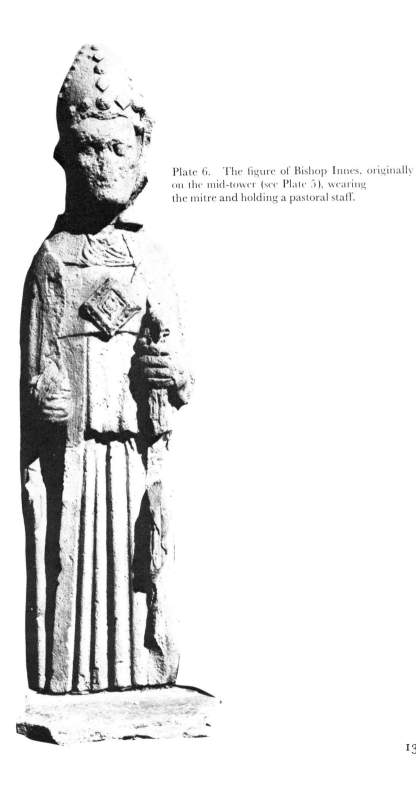

Plate 6. The figure of Bishop Innes, originally
on the mid-tower (see Plate 5), wearing
the mitre and holding a pastoral staff.

## Transepts

The transepts are the oldest part of the edifice. Each transept contained two chapels; the most northerly was dedicated to Saint Thomas à Becket of Canterbury and the two in the south transept to Saint Peter and Saint Paul. The lower parts of the western walls of the transepts have been arcaded. The south transept has a doorway in the south wall at the south-west angle and above it is a small

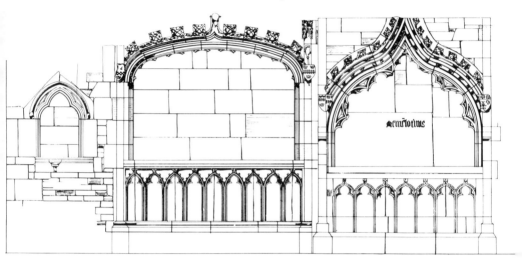

Plate 7. The architectural detail of the tombs in the south transept. Both have panelled fronts and the canopies above have crockets (regularly-spaced decoration carved in formalised leaf shapes). On each side of the canopies are heraldic shields.

The easternmost tomb (to left) is that of Bishop James Stewart (1460–1462); his coat of arms with pastoral staff is at the head. Patterns of vine and oak leaves and acorns adorn the canopy. The bishop's effigy is lost: the effigy in a coat of mail now lying within the recess belonged to the tomb of Robert Innes of Invermarkie which originally stood in the Chapel of St Peter, at the crossing. The jupon, or short surcoat, bears the three stars from the Innes coat of arms.

The west tomb (to right) has an unidentified coat of arms at its head and at the foot an impaled shield with the Stewart arms. The recess contains a recumbent effigy in the military costume of the mid fifteenth century and the words *memeto finis* (in memory of the end) are cut on the back of the tomb.

To the east of the tombs (extreme left of plate) is a piscina, or stone basin for washing the Communion or Mass vessels. Near the piscina, on the wall (not shown on plate) is a consecration cross.

Plate 8. *opposite* The gable of the south transept.

vesica-shaped window furnished with stone window-seats suggesting that there was a room at this level on the western side of the transept. To the east of the doorway there are two mural tombs, both insertions of fifteenth-century date (Plate 7).

The south exterior elevation (Plate 8) is well proportioned, the vertical lines of buttresses and the steep pitch of the surmounting gable tending to accentuate its height. The ingoes of the narrow

doorway carried three columns with detached shafts. The caps on the west side are boldly cut in a pattern of leaf-and-berry, while those on the opposite side portray a leaf pattern of more simple character. A large-scale 'dog-tooth' ornament enriches the mouldings of the arched head. The lower windows are lancets and those of the clerestory are round-headed and have nook shafts. Above in the gable were three graduated lancets contained within a semi-circular arch. There were one large lancet and two clerestory lancets in the west wall and in the east wall there was a lancet over each altar, with clerestory above.

The architectural treatment of the north transept was similar to that of the south but in place of a doorway leading to the outside there was a stairway in the corresponding angle. This led to the clerestory passage and the wall-walk and provided the first stage of approach to the wall-head of the mid-tower. St Thomas à Becket's Chapel was the burial-place of the family of Dunbar. The tomb recesses have been destroyed, but two effigies remain. The jupon of the warrior in armour (fifteenth century) bears the three cushions lozengeways for Dunbar. The other figure, vested in a long flowing gown and cloak, is of earlier date and is now defaced. The foot-rest of this effigy is carved with a representation of the 'lion and the lamb'. On the west wall is a mural tablet of post-Reformation date; it is in the early classic Renaissance style and is a memorial to the family of Dunbar of Bennetfield.


## Choir

The choir screen or pulpitum, probably constructed of stone, stretched across the kirk under the eastern arch of the crossing. The oak choir stalls for the secular canons occupied the space immed-iately to the east of the pulpitum and extended along the walls. The bishop's throne was situated at the east end of the southern range of stalls and at the base of the large pier. Parts of the mouldings of the pier and of the arch springing from its western side have been cut away to accommodate the throne which was furnished with an elaborately carved canopy. It is of interest to note that the mason who removed the mouldings was careful to decorate the ends of their sections. The first choir and presbytery together occupied the total space of the present choir and the first high altar stood just westward of a line drawn between the north and south mid-piers. These piers terminate in a 'spire'-like design of three storeys. The lower two-thirds of the north wall is part of the earliest building. At the base a discoloured band of masonry testifies to the damage done by the fire of the first burning. Above this the wall has been repaired and

Plate 9. The choir and presbytery seen from the crossing in 1826. The bent and sturdy figure of John Shanks, the first custodian of the cathedral (see page 44) stands in the middle of the foreground group. From *A series of views . . . of Elgin Cathedral* (1826).

altered and on it can be traced the outline of an inner arcading similar to that of the clerestory windows of the south wall of the transept. The clerestory windows and passage above were formed when the choir was extended. The large blue-limestone slab, lying on the floor near the arcade which opens to the south aisle, contained a

Plate 10. The choir and presbytery from the south, from R. W. Billings, *The Baronial and Ecclesiastical Antiquities of Scotland*, 1845–52.

great brass plate on which was engraved the figure of a bishop set within a niche surmounted by an elaborate canopy and bearing an inscription, the engraved lines of the whole design being infilled with black, red and white mastic. This monument was imported from one of the famous Franco-Flemish workshops of the City of Tournai and the stone came from a Tournai quarry. The slightly sunk channels on the stone indicate the positions of the strips of metal which backed the brass at the joints of the plates, and the small holes filled with lead held the pins which attached the brass to the stone setting. The remains of another Tournai monument are to be seen in the floor of St Mary's Aisle.

From the early fourteenth century until the time of the Reformation many fine monumental brasses were imported into Scotland from Flanders but all that remain of these are a few of the Tournai stone slabs in which the brasses were set.

## Sculptured Cross-slab

At the west end of the choir and on its north side is a Pictish cross-slab which was unearthed near St Giles' Kirk. On the front is a cross standing on a rectangular base and ornamented with an interlaced pattern now much defaced. In the four angles of the cross are figures probably representing the four Evangelists, while the space below is occupied by an interlaced design with four animal heads meeting in

Plate 11. Pictish cross-slab, probably ninth century AD. The cross is on the front of the slab. On the back, shown here, is a spirited hunting scene and, above it, two of the enigmatic symbols used by the Picts: a double disc and Z-shaped rod, and a crescent and V-shaped rod.

the centre. On the back of the slab is a spirited hunting scene surmounted by Pictish symbols (Plate 11). The stone may have been carved in the ninth century.

## Presbytery

The presbytery is a fine example of late thirteenth-century or First Pointed Gothic architecture. It was abundantly lighted by a well-arranged group of windows in the east gable (Plate 12), in addition to twin side-windows and a clerestory range of singular beauty. The lower windows of the east elevation had traceried heads and those in the north and south walls three lights and traceried heads.

The floor is stepped at three levels; the High Altar stood on the highest of these and close to the east wall. The arcaded sedilia contain seats for four ecclesiastics arranged in successive tiers. The under side of the canopy takes the form of 'dwarf vaulting' and the terminal finials are ornamented with a flower pattern. There is no trace of the piscina but it probably occupied a position on the sill of the window immediately to the east of the sedilia. In the north wall is a recessed mural tomb with a cusped arched canopy and a crocketted gable. This feature is not an insertion but part of the presbytery design and

Plate 12.   The east front.

was probably made for Bishop Archibald (1253–1299). Another bishop's monument is contained within the arcade which gives access to the north aisle. The canopy, which consisted of three crocketted gablets with tall finials, extended across the arcade, the westernmost gablet being set over an opening connecting the presbytery with the aisle. The remaining gablets covered the tomb-chest, which has long since been removed. The effigy which rested under the canopy was probably that now lying in a mural recess in the north wall in the second 'bay' of the south choir aisle. Consecration crosses are to be seen on the walls of the presbytery.

## Aisles

To the south of the choir is St Mary's Aisle. It is the burial place of Bishop Winchester (1436–1460), Bishop Tulloch (1477–1482) and the Gordons of Huntly. Probably on account of its connection with the Gordon family this aisle has not been allowed to become totally ruinous. The rib-and-panel vaulting with carved bosses illustrates the nature of the ceilings which covered the corresponding aisle on the north side of the choir, the north aisles and part of the south aisles of the nave. The subjects carved on the bosses are typical of the period (thirteenth century); for instance, the representations of dragons and salamanders which writhe and twist among the foliage. Immediately under the east windows are the remains of an altar; part of the window-sill above it has been cut away to make room for a retable. To the north of this altar is the mural tomb of Bishop Winchester, the best preserved of the pre-Reformation monuments (Plates 13 and 14).

The tomb recess in the second bay of the aisle is of fifteenth-century date and in it lies a fourteenth-century effigy of a bishop in eucharistic vestments, probably removed from the monument in the arcade on the north side of the presbytery. The foot-rest is carved with the 'lion and lamb' motif and the canopy of the niche which encloses the figure bears on its dexter side the royal arms of Scotland and on the sinister side the arms of Moray. The figure probably represents Bishop John Pilmore (1326–1362). In the centre of the aisle and over the burial vault of the Gordons is the monument of the first Lord Huntly. The effigy, now defaced, is shown in the robe of the Lord Chancellor of Scotland with a poniard hanging from the girdle. The inscription round the bevelled edge of the slab on which the effigy rests reads:

*hic iacet nobilis et potens dñs alexāder gordone primus comes de huntlie dñs de gordone et badzenoth qui obiit apud huntlie 15 iulii anno dñi 1470*

Here lies the noble and powerful lord Alexander Gordon first Earl of Huntly Lord of Gordon and Badenoch who died at Huntly 15 July AD 1470

Plate 13.   Tomb of Bishop of Winchester. The ogee (double-curved) arch of the recess is decorated with crockets, like stylised flowers, above and cusps below. The ornamental buttresses flanking the tomb carry shields on which were painted the coat of arms of the bishop. The inscription in Gothic lettering is on the sloping edge of the cover of the panelled tomb-chest. Part of it has been cut out in relief—the rest is left unfinished. In 1938, when the inscription was clearer, it appeared to read:

*hic jacet recolende memo$^e$ johanes Winnechestair dns epus moravien: q*
*obiit xxii die mee Apl Ano dni. Mccclx.*

here lies John Winchester lord bishop of Moray, of distinguished memory, who died on the 20th day of the month of April in the year of our Lord 1460.

On the underside of the arched recess are to be seen contemporary drawings in black and red line of four censing angels. It is probable that the whole monument was coloured. The recumbent figure of the bishop (see also Plate 13) is dressed as for the celebrations of Communion. The mitred head rests on a pillow and the sandalled feet on a lion. The long pastoral staff lies on the left side of the figure with the crook in line with the face.

This is an example of the early use of Arabic numerals in Scotland. The Earl's full achievement of arms appears on the south side of the tomb; underneath is the motto 'Byd-And'.

The recumbent figure in armour which lies on a composite pedestal is that of De le Hay of Lochloy (Plate 15) but it is not in its original position. The heraldry is displayed on the jupon, as it is in the case of the contemporary effigies of Innes and Dunbar. This inscription reads:

*hic jacet wills de le hay quōdā dñs de lochloy qui obiit viii die mēs decebris año dñi mcccc xxii ate piciet*

Here lies William de le Hay sometime Lord of Lochloy who died the 8 day of the month of December AD 1422 for whose soul may God be propitiated

Set into the aisled floor are several grave-slabs from the tombs of ecclesiastics. These bear their respective heraldic shields, a cross on a stepped base, a chalice with paten, a service book. The following personages are commemorated: a rector of Rothes called Leslie who died in 1520; Thomas Leslie, rector of Kingussie, who died 8th May, 1525; Thomas Caldar, a precentor of Ross, who died 8th September, 1519; James Lochart (1480) and his brother Robert, Cantor

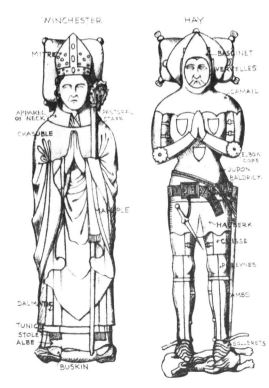

Plate 14. The effigy of Bishop Winchester: from a drawing by Dr J. S. Richardson.

Plate 15. The effigy of William de la Hay: from a drawing by Dr J. S. Richardson.

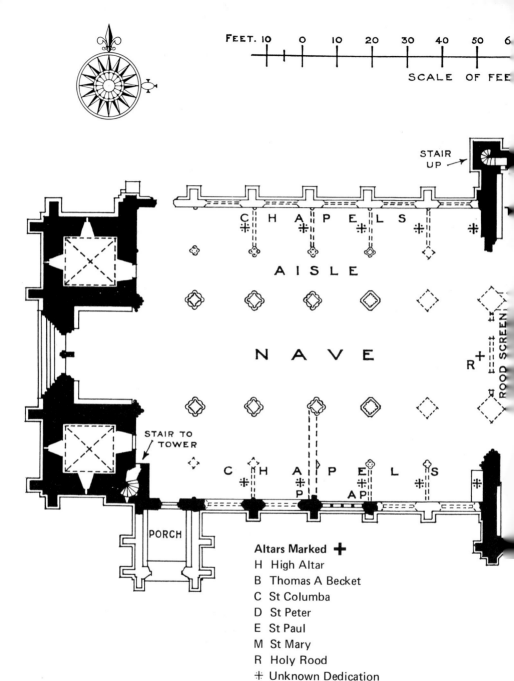

FEET. 10   0   10   20   30   40   50  6

SCALE OF FEE

STAIR UP

C H A P E L S

A I S L E

N A V E

ROOD SCREEN

R

STAIR TO TOWER

C H A P E L S

P

AP

S

PORCH

**Altars Marked ✙**
H  High Altar
B  Thomas A Becket
C  St Columba
D  St Peter
E  St Paul
M  St Mary
R  Holy Rood
✝  Unknown Dedication

A  Denotes Aumbry
P  Denotes Piscina
S  Denotes Sedilia

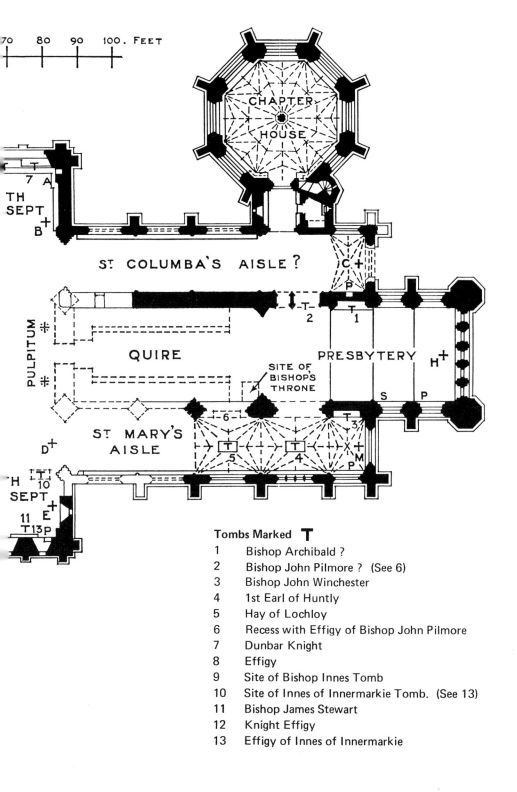

70　80　90　100. FEET

CHAPTER HOUSE

7 A

TH SEPT

B +

ST COLUMBA'S AISLE ?

C +

P

PULPITUM

QUIRE

T 2

T 1

PRESBYTERY

H +

SITE OF BISHOP'S THRONE

S　P

ST MARY'S AISLE

D +

6

T 5

T 4

T 3

X +

M

P

H SEPT

T 10

11　E +

T 13 P

**Tombs Marked T**

1　Bishop Archibald ?
2　Bishop John Pilmore ?　(See 6)
3　Bishop John Winchester
4　1st Earl of Huntly
5　Hay of Lochloy
6　Recess with Effigy of Bishop John Pilmore
7　Dunbar Knight
8　Effigy
9　Site of Bishop Innes Tomb
10　Site of Innes of Innermarkie Tomb.　(See 13)
11　Bishop James Stewart
12　Knight Effigy
13　Effigy of Innes of Innermarkie

(Singer). Two monuments of this type, removed for protection from St Mary's Aisle to the ground-floor chamber of the western tower, commemorate William Lyel, sub-deacon of Moray, who died 1504, and James Leslye, rector of Kingussie and Rothes, who died March 1547. Most of the post-Reformation grave-slabs are memorials to members of the Gordon family and display their coat of arms. There are also slabs commemorating Donald Irvine and Elizabeth Gordon, 1623; Lucretia Gordon, 'spous to George Cumine', sometime Provost of Elgin, who died 1668; Alex. Gordoune of Strathawin (1622) and William Caldar of Spynie, a Provost of Elgin, who died in 1690. Set on the south wall between the two easternmost windows is an eighteenth-century grey-and-white marble monument displaying the portrait bust in bas-relief of Henrietta Duchess of Gordon, a daughter of Charles Mordaunt, Earl of Peterburgh, who died in 1760.

The north choir aisle is very ruinous; the easternmost bay only is now vaulted. There is a piscina in its south wall.

## Chapter-House

A vestibule which was ceiled with a rib-and-panel vault leads from the north aisle to the much-altered thirteenth-century chapter-house. The entrance had twin doorways with a traceried head. The small sacristy (?), with its slightly ornamented basin, was entered by a doorway in the east wall of the passage; it is of fifteenth-century

Plate 16.   The octagonal chapter-house and the east end of the cathedral.

date. The construction of the chamber has necessitated the closing up of a window in the north aisle. The chapter-house doorway has carved caps of early design and 'dog-tooth' enrichment. This is original work but the inner mouldings and the detail of the doorway within belong to the reconstruction period. The chapter-house is octagonal in plan; originally it was ceiled in timber but after the 1390 fire the central pillar of stone and the rib-and-panel vault of highly developed design were introduced. The traceried windows were remodelled to a smaller size and the walls within the building were repaired with the exception of the area over the entrance doorway. Immediately to the east of the entrance is a small doorway giving access to a wheel-stair leading to the roof chamber. Facing the entrance there are five canopied seats which were occupied by the high dignitaries of the Cathedral Chapter while plain stone benching to accommodate other members of the Chapter is carried round the remaining walls below the windows. The interior is enriched with stone carvings many of which are of interest to the archaeologist or to the lover of the works of the medieval sculptor. Oak leaves and acorns, grapes and vine leaves decorate the corbels of the arcaded seats. Odd 'animals' and amusing 'humans', including a jester, support the angle shafts. Grimacing demon-faces look down from the corbels set high in the window ingoes, while one of these

Plate 17. The elaborate vault of the chapter-house springing from a central pillar.

window corbels depicts a fox habited as a friar and holding a stole, preaching to the geese, and another a gowned dwarf with a conical hat, seated on a chair, holding a large flagon in his right hand and the leaf of a tree in the left. The moulded pillar has a lectern supported by two 'angels'. The moulded cap of the pillar bears an oak-leaf enrichment, the Royal Arms of Scotland surmounted by a crown, a shield with the emblems of the Passion, the coat of arms

Plate 18. Figure sculpture in the chapter-house: Christ in Majesty.

of Bishop Andrew Stuart (1482–1501) surmounted by a mitre, a shield charged with the Five Wounds of Christ, the Cross and the Crown of Thorns; St Andrew on his cross; the Royal Arms; a shield charged with the Five Wounds. The vaulting of the chapter-house is of stellar pattern and contains twenty-four carved bosses. Of these, eight are grotesque human masks; eight leaf or flower patterns; and the others a Christ in Majesty (Plate 18) set within a vesica-shaped panel, a figure of a bishop holding a pastoral staff, his right hand raised in blessing, the Royal Arms surmounted by a crown, a dragon, a shield portraying the emblems of Our Lord's Passion: the cross, crown of thorns, spear, reed with hissop, pillar and scourge, seamless coat, ladder, dice, nails, hammer, pincers, lantern and cock.

The late seventeenth-century tombstones of Episcopalian bishops and their families in the chapter-house do not belong to the Cathedral but were brought there from St Giles' Parish Kirk when the latter was demolished in 1826.

Plate 19. Tombstone of John Geddes (page 30).

The external masonry of the chapter-house is that of the original building and the outline of its windows can be seen surrounding the masonry of the later window insertions. The corbels of the window hood-mouldings are nearly all of the grotesque human-mask variety, but those of the restored window are 'animal'. To complete the design of the chapter-house on the outside a roof of pyramidal form would require to be added.

## Burial Ground

In the burial ground to the south are the remains of the 'bishop's cross' with its socket stone. Late seventeenth and eighteenth century burial enclosures were built against the graveyard walls and a few typical examples of these have been retained as records of a past burial custom. There are numerous grave slabs and memorials to members of the Glovers' Guild exhibiting their heraldic achievement: the cutter surmounted by St Crispin's crown and by the symbols of their trade and the shears. Two such memorials in the south wall are of particular interest.

One, dated 1679, is that of James Young, glover, burgess in Elgin, and his family. Besides the emblems of his craft an hour-glass and a clock are depicted. On the central panel, between them is the injunction 'FEAR . GOD . O . MORTAL . MAN: WHAT . ART . THOW . DOEING: REMEMBER . THY . EARANT: FOR . THY . GLAS . IS . RWNING:' and the surrounding panels are also inscribed.

The other, dated 1687, commemorates the family of John Geddes (Plate 19), another member of the same guild, and again portrays the glove and shears. A motto, 'GRACE ME GUID, IN HOPE I BYDE', appears on the scroll, and in the panel under the inscription is the following verse:

THIS WORLD IS A CITE
FULL OF STREETS . &
DEATH IS THE MERCAT
THAT ALL MEN MEETS
IF LYFE WERE A THING
THAT MONIE COULD
BUY . THE POOR COULD
NOT LIVE & THE RICH
WOULD NOT DIE.

# HISTORY

Plate 20.   Early fifteenth-century boss, probably from one of the aisle vaults.

At the beginning of the twelfth century, Scotland as we know it scarcely existed; in no sense of the word was there a Scottish nation. Instead there was a group of large provinces—Moravia, Cat, Argyle, Galloway—centres in more or less resolute hostility to the unifying pressure of the Scottish Crown.

With the advent of King Alexander I (1106–1124) the first serious efforts for the unification and pacification of Scotland, other than by the sword, were begun. In the first year of his reign in June

1107 the Bishopric of Moray was founded, as also were those of St Andrews and of Dunkeld.

Alexander, it may be mentioned, was the first of the Scottish kings to promote trading facilities in the North; possibly the knowledge that the religious institutions of the period developed commerce in their neighbourhood may have had something to do with the granting of these facilities, for trading communities meant men, and men were useful in time of war.

David I (1124–1153) confirmed these trading facilities and developed them by founding the Priory of Urquhart in 1125 and the Abbey of Kinloss in 1151. During his reign loyal and wealthy Anglo-Norman barons and others, peaceably inclined, were induced to settle in the province and it was only during the reign of Malcolm IV (1153–1165) that the great territorial district of Moravia came to an end as a separate entity.

Unfortunately, the original muniments pertaining to the first three centuries of the Bishopric were burned along with the Cathedral itself in 1390. Such charters etc. as are recorded in the 'Register of the Bishoprick of Moray', a parchment volume of 169 leaves preserved in the National Library of Scotland, were undoubtedly collected in pursuance of a Papal Commission issued in 1394. These records are far from complete, hence the paucity of our early information. This Register, transcribed and edited by Sheriff Cosmo Innes, was published by the Bannatyne Club in 1837 under the title 'Registrum Episcopatus Moraviensis'.

Gregorius, a monk, is mentioned as the first Bishop of Moray. We have no records of the struggle in the province between the ancient Pictish Church of the Culdees and the Roman Church but it is probable that Gregorius may have been a leading monk in the earlier Church and that by his being promoted—as in Dunkeld and in Ireland—the Roman Church was enabled gradually to strangle the individuality of the Culdees and take over their places of worship, sites consecrated by an immemorial series of religious services.

Birnie, a known Culdee foundation, was the seat of the diocese during the rule of the first four bishops—Gregorius, William (1158–1161), who was Papal Legate in Scotland in 1160, Felix (1162–1171), in whose favour deeds are first recorded, and Simon de Tonei (1171–1184). For a short period during the time of Richard (1187–1203) its place was taken by Kinnedar, another Culdee centre. Thereafter Spynie—still another Culdee centre—became the seat of the diocese, suggesting the gradual absorption of the older forms of religion.

Richard was the first of the Bishops about whom we know anything. He was a special favourite of King William the Lion (1165–1214), to whom he had been chaplain. King William frequently resided within the diocese and besides enjoining that 'my Bailiffs of Moray . . . shall yearly make good the full and entire said tenth of my returns to Bishop Richard and his successors', he heaped upon the See great gifts of land. It is worthy of note that the ancient possessions of the Church consisted, not of tithes alone, but of lands

Plate 21. Early 15th century head, probably the stop or terminal of a moulding above an opening or recess.

scattered over the province and in view of the condition of the country at that period it was undoubtedly a step towards pacification to throw such property into the hands of those whose duty it was to inculcate peace.

Richard foresaw that the old province was entering upon a period of prosperity through the settlement of the aforesaid barons, such as Freskinus de Moravia and Berowald de Innes, in conjunction with those descendants of the old Celtic families who had embraced the new order. If he did not actually conceive the idea of transforming the Church of the Holy Trinity, which stood a little to the north-east of the Elgin of that date, into a building worthy of being the Cathedral Kirk of the diocese, he certainly furthered it, and in this he had the support of King William's princely gifts. William the Lion was otherwise a great benefactor to the province. He confirmed to his burgesses in Moray their 'free hanse'—the right of free trade—

33

and his charters are full of expressions of protection and regard for them.

Bishop Bricius Douglas (1203–1223), who was residing at Spynie early in his incumbency, applied to Pope Innocent III to have the Cathedral of the See, previously undefined, to be fixed at the 'Sancte Trinitatis de Spyny' and by a Papal Bull issued in April 1207, the Bishops of St Andrews and Brechin with others were appointed to carry out the consecration services, which they did. The foundations of this Church were traceable until recent years. They showed a building of simple character with walls partly clay-built, the dimensions being 22.6 m (74 ft) long and 10.7 m (35 ft) wide.

Bricius Douglas was a very talented and energetic prelate. He founded a College of Canons, eight in number, gave his Cathedral a Constitution founded on the usage of Lincoln, and in other directions laid the foundations of the glorious future of the bishopric. Yet almost immediately after the consecration at Spynie we find him, with the King's sanction, imploring the Pope to have the Cathedral transferred from Spynie to the Church of the Holy Trinity *'juxta Elgyn'*. The translation was, however, granted only in the first year of the incumbency of his successor Bishop Andrew (1224–1242), and in July 1224 the impressive service of consecration was performed by Gilbert, Bishop of Caithness, and the Church of the Holy Trinity *'juxta Elgyn'* was transformed into the Cathedral Church of the diocese of Moray.

Bishop Andrew was a scion of the powerful family of de Moravia, whose descendants are still of the highest rank in Scotland. He had been one of the two delegates sent to Lincoln by Bishop Bricius and as he had all the ecclesiastical ambition of his predecessor, the magnificence of Lincoln Cathedral had doubtless fired his imagination. Thanks to growing revenues and to truly splendid endowments from his relatives of Duffus and Petty, Andrew was in a position to embellish and enrich his Cathedral. He was the more able to carry out improvements through the liberality of Elgin's greatest benefactor, King Alexander II (1214–1249), who made large gifts to the Cathedral and was responsible further for the founding of the Maison Dieu, the Black Friars, the Grey Friars and Pluscarden Priory. He also founded a chaplaincy within the Cathedral for the soul of King Duncan.

Andrew was an outstanding prelate of whom we would gladly know more. He increased the Chapter or College of Canons from eight to twenty-three—seven dignitaries, sixteen canons—of which numbers it consisted for some 300 years. At this time it is recorded there were twenty-two vicars-choral and about as many chaplains.

Bishop Andrew died in 1242 and his remains were deposited in the south side of the choir under the large stone of blue marble.

The Cathedral then consisted of a choir and presbytery, a crossing surmounted by a tower, north and south transepts, an aisled nave and two massive western towers. With the exception of the ground floors of the western towers no part of the original Kirk was vaulted with stone. The roofing and the spires were of timber, covered with lead.

Plate 22. Early fifteenth-century boss, probably from one of the aisle vaults.

Soon after the completion of the building the three eastern 'bays' of the south aisle of the nave were extended southwards, the long arm of the transept permitting the double aisle formation.

In a short history it is inadvisable to detail the Chapter as fully constituted with the ecclesiastical titles and country residential privileges of its Canons. The Bishops' palaces or castles were at Birnie, Kinnedar and Spynie. The manses and gardens of the other dignitaries and canons clustered round the Cathedral, all enclosed within a strong precinct wall of stone 2 m broad, about 3.7 m high and some 823 m in circuit, parts of which still exist, and thus they formed a distinct community known as the 'Collegium' or Chanonry. Two of the manses are still inhabited, the Dean's now the College, and the Archdeacon's—the South College.

The area of the diocese coincided roughly with that of the old province. It extended on the north along the Moray Firth from the Spey to Ross-shire, on the west it included the country adjoining Loch Ness with the valleys of the Nairn and Findhorn, on the south Badenoch and Strathspey with the valleys of the Avon and the

Fiddich, on the east a part of Banffshire, including Strathisla, Strath-
bogie in Aberdeenshire and stretching thence to the Spey about
Fochabers.

The next three Bishops—Simon (1242–1252), Ralph, who died
before consecration, and Archibald (1253–1298), who chose
Kinnedar Castle for his residence—have left no particular records
of their incumbencies. During this half-century two misfortunes befell
the Cathedral. In 1244 it received some considerable injury, no one
knows what, and in 1270, according to Fordoun, it was damaged by
fire—which must have been very disastrous as well as wilful, the
manses also having been burned.

Evidence of this destruction is to be seen on the east sides of the
western towers immediately above the water-tabling of the timber
roofs of the original aisles. A great rebuilding now took place; the
Kirk was enlarged to its present dimensions and a chapter-house was
built. The nave was completed with double aisles on both sides,

introducing a French feature of cathedral planning. The aisles in the westernmost 'bay' were provided with doorways, that in the south wall having a projecting porch. The choir and presbytery were doubled in length and provided with north and south stone-vaulted aisles of five bays. The chapter-house was built to the north and was connected with the north choir aisle by a vestibule. Thus, at the close of the thirteenth century, in distant Moray a great masterpiece of ecclesiastical architecture was brought into being.

David de Moravia (1299–1326), who succeeded, stands out as a strong and commanding individual like all the other recorded members of the family. He was one of the chief leaders in the North during the War of Independence and to quote E M Barron, 'When Andrew de Moray fell covered with wounds and glory his uncle David de Moravia, Bishop of Moray, took up his work and carried it on with a thoroughness, a devotion, a courage and a singleness of purpose to which there is no parallel in the history of the War'. He was excommunicated by order of Edward I of England and fled to Norway, returning to the diocese after Edward's death in 1307. Bishop David died in 1325 and was buried in the choir. He bequeathed funds for the benefit of four poor scholars from Moray studying in Paris, the beginnings of an institution which later became known as The Scots College at Paris and which was administered by the Bishops of Moray till the Reformation.

John Pilmore (1326–1362) was the next Bishop. He was succeeded by Alexander Bur (1362–1397), during whose old age fearful destruction fell upon the Cathedral. Alexander Stewart, Earl of Buchan and Lord of Badenoch, the second son of King Robert II, known for his fierceness as the 'Wolf of Badenoch', having a quarrel with the bishop who had excommunicated him, swooped down from his stronghold at Lochindorb in May 1390 and with his 'wyld Wykked Heland-men burned the town of Forres, the choir of the Church of St Laurence there also the manse of the Archdeacon, and in the month of June following in the Feast of the Blessed Botulph Abbot he burned the whole town of Elgin, 18 noble and beautiful manses of Canons and Chaplains and what was further still more cursed and lamentable the noble and highly adored Church of Moray with all the books Charters and other valuable things of the country therein kept'.

This crime nearly broke the heart of the aged prelate and his petition to King Robert III to assist towards the rebuilding, is pitiful in its pathos: 'My church was the ornament of the realm, the glory of the kingdom, the delight of foreigners and stranger guests; an object of praise and glorification in foreign realms by reason of the multitude of those serving and the beauty of its ornament and in

Plate 24. The destruction of Elgin Cathedral in 1390; by the 'Wolf of Badenoch': an imaginative 19th-century drawing.

which we believe God was rightly worshipped; not to speak of its high belfries, its ancient furniture and its innumerable jewels'. The letter was written immediately after the burning of the Cathedral and chapter-house by the 'Wolf of Badenoch'.

Once again the damage caused by conflagration necessitated extensive repairs and rebuilding and a re-roofing of the western part of the nave. The gable wall above the western portal was taken down, reconstructed and given a large traceried window and the doorways of the portal were remodelled. The main piers of the arcading of the western part of the nave were renewed and a new roof was provided. The crossing and mid-tower were rebuilt and new tracery was made for the wheel window in the east gable of the presbytery. The intense heat caused by the burning of the chapter-house roof so damaged the masonry that the interior of the building had to be refaced. New traceried windows were provided and a central stone pillar with a rib-and-panel vaulted ceiling was introduced. The King made an annual contribution and the general response to the appeal must have been substantial for when Alexander Macdonald, son of the Lord of the Isles, 'spulzied' the Chanonry in July 1402, during the time of Bishop Spynie (1397–1406), the plunder was rich enough to entice him to return in the following October. But this time he was met at the west precinct gate by the Bishop and Canons who, in short, 'so worked upon the feelings of Alexander and his Captains that they confessed their faults and earnestly begged to be absolved'.

John Innes succeeded in 1407 and ruled seven years. On his death the Chapter met and bound themselves that whoever should be elected Bishop should annually apply one third of his revenue in repairing the Cathedral until all should be completed. Bishop Leighton, who was consecrated in 1414, was translated to Aberdeen in 1422. David succeeded and held office until 1429. He is omitted from some lists and there is obscurity about his episcopate. Columba de Dunbar, younger son of George, tenth Earl of March, and a nephew of the Earl of Moray, was then promoted to the See. The year of his consecration is doubtful but he was Bishop in 1429. In 1433 there is a record of a safe-conduct permitting him to pass through England on his way to Rome and another the following year when he journeyed to the Council of Basle. He died in 1435.

In John Winchester we have a real and vivid personality. He came to Scotland in the suite of King James I, with whom he was in high favour. He was successively appointed Prebendary of Dunkeld, Provost of Lincluden, Lord Clerk-Register, and in 1437 he was consecrated Bishop of Moray. King James employed him in various State affairs, including that of Master of Works. It was during his time that the lands of the Church were erected into the Barony of Spynie with full Regality rights. The temporal influence of the Bishops of Moray was now growing much more luxuriantly than their spiritual. Bishop Winchester died in 1458 and was buried in St Mary's Aisle.

James Stewart of the family of Strathavon, Lord High Treasurer, succeeded in 1458 and died in 1460. He was followed by his brother David in 1461. David excommunicated the first Earl of Huntly for resisting payment of rents. Irritated by this, the Earl threatened to pluck the Bishop out of his pigeon-holes in scorn of the mean dwelling at Spynie at that date. But the haughty prelate, who was rebuilding, rejoined that he should by and by have a nest that the Earl and all his clan should not be able to pluck him out of, and the great tower at Spynie Palace known as 'Davy's' tower, although much shattered today, survives to show that the Bishop's reply was no empty boast. David Stewart died in 1475.

William Tulloch, Keeper of the Privy Seal, previously Bishop of Orkney, was translated to Moray in 1477 and appears to have been more of a politician than a cleric. He was one of the ambassadors to Denmark to negotiate the marriage of James III and the 'Lady Margaret', an alliance which placed the Orkney and Shetland Islands in the possession of the Scottish Crown. He died in 1482. Andrew Stewart, third son of the Black Knight of Lorn and of his lady, the widow of James I, was the next Bishop (1482–1501). He held various high appointments, including that of Keeper of the Privy Seal.

He was succeeded by Andrew Forman (1501–1514), one of the most accomplished and successful diplomats of his age. He was a great pluralist, being Commendator of the Abbeys of Dryburgh and Pittenweem and of Cottingham in England (the commendator of a benefice drew its revenues without being obliged to perform any duties). King James IV appointed him Ambassador to England, and later to France. From thence he went to Rome, and for the triumph of his diplomacy Pope Julius II appointed him Papal Legate for Scotland. He was nominated Archbishop of Bruges, but in 1514 was exchanged to St Andrews.

With James Hepburn (1516–1523) the bishopric appears to have reached its zenith of wealth and magnificence. He was the third son of Adam, Lord Hailes, and brother of Patrick, first Earl of Bothwell, and among other high offices held that of King's Lord Treasurer.

Bishop Schaw (1524–1527) had the character of a man of great virtue. He also was Ambassador to England. Alexander Stewart, who succeeded in 1527, was the son of Alexander, Duke of Albany, son of King James II. He was the first Prior of Whithorn, but not much is known of him. He died in 1535. With Patrick Hepburn (1535–1573), son of the first Earl of Bothwell, we come to the last Roman Catholic Bishop of Moray. He had been Prior of St Andrews and was Commendator of the Abbacy of Scone.

Bishop Hepburn was one of the commissioners who negotiated the marriage of Mary Queen of Scots with the Dauphin of France. During his incumbency there took place within the Cathedral a

Plate 25. Early fifteenth-century boss, probably from one of the aisle vaults.

fight, known as 'The Bloody Vespers', between two powerful families in Moray, those of Innes and Dunbar. On 1st January 1555 William Innes of that ilk and 32 others with 80 followers, all armed and 'of ancient feud and forethought felony', came to the service with intent 'for the slauchters' of Alexander Dunbar, Prior of Pluscarden, David Dunbar, Dean of Moray, and sundry Dunbar laymen. By a remarkable coincidence James Dunbar of Tarbert and 12 others, with 60 Dunbar followers, had also come under cover of night with the intention of killing the Laird of Innes and his servants. The scene of violence and bloodshed may be imagined and as an aggravation of the offence the murderous onset was made 'in the presence of the Holy Sacrament'. Beyond several 'hurtings' we know little of the fight, certainly it was not decisive for the feud was kept going for a further twenty years. Wise in his generation, Patrick Hepburn early realised that the Reformation was not a matter to be opposed, by spiritual weapons at any rate, and by 1540 he had begun the alienation of Church lands thus providing for his future maintenance and that of his numerous family. When the storm burst in 1560 he was in a position not merely to be brave but to defy the Reformation. Shutting himself within the Palace of Spynie he carried on his unprincipled life until his death in June 1573.

The last public celebration of Mass within the Cathedral took place a whole generation after the Papal authority had been proscribed. After the Battle of Glenlivet on 4th October, 1594, when the leaders of the Catholic forces, the Earls of Huntly and Errol, had defeated the Government forces under Argyle, the party realised that it had no outside support. The Earls and their adherents, it is recorded, assembled within the Cathedral at Elgin to discuss the situation. After Mass had been celebrated James Gordon, a Jesuit priest and uncle to Huntly, descended from the high altar and from the steps of the chancel implored his kinsman and friends to remain in their own land and hazard all for their faith. It was in vain. The spirit of the Gordons and Hays was broken and early in 1595 Errol embarked at Peterhead for the Continent, as did Huntly at Aberdeen.

The story of the decadence of the Cathedral is painful. Through Bishop Hepburn's profuse alienation of its property no Church funds remained for its upkeep. It was never used by Presbyterian ministers nor by the bishops introduced into the Reformed Church and not being a parish church none claimed the responsibility of maintaining it. The lead roofing was stripped by order of the Regent Moray and his Privy Council in 1567 and although two years later they spoke of restoration the Regent's murder must have put a stop to the good intention. With the dispersal of the remnants of the Catholic influence in the district after the Battle of Glenlivet it would appear from the Records of the Kirk Session of Elgin that the Cathedral (or Chanonry Kirk as it is therein designated) and burial ground had indeed fallen on evil days. The Minute of 21 December, 1599, reads: 'Anent the Chanonrie Kirk—All profane pastyme inhibited to be usitt by any persones ather within the burgh or college and speciallie futballing through the toun, snaw balling, singing of carrellis or uther prophane sangis, guysing, pypying, violing, and dansing and speciallie all thir aboue specifeit forbiddin in the Chanonrie kirk or kirk yaird thairoff (except futball). All women and lassis forbidden to haunt or resoirt their under the paynis of publict repentans, at the leist during this tyme quhilk is superstitiouslie keippet fra the XXV day of December to the last of Januar nixt thairaftir quhilk ordinance the minister sall intimat furt out of the pulpitt'. For fully fifty years after this inhibitions of a like nature and anent the haunting of the Chanonry Kirk by the superstitious is recorded.

With the roofs exposed the elements gradually worked destruction. In December 1637 the choir rafters were blown down. John Taylor, 'the water poet', an Englishman who visited Elgin in 1618, narrates in his journal, 'I went to Elgen in Murray, an ancient citie, where there stood a faire and beautiful church with three steeples, the walls of it and the steeples all yet standing; but the roofs, windowes and many marble monuments and tombes of honourable and worthie personages all broken and defaced: this was done in the time when ruine bare rule and Knox knocked doune churches'. Although lacking the protection of the roof 'for several score years', the painted timber rood-screen with the great painting of the Crucifixion which was framed in the arch over the loft remained in excellent con-

Plate 26.   Early fifteenth-century boss, probably from one of the aisle vaults.

dition until it was taken down and destroyed in 1640 by a minister of Elgin named Gilbert Ross. The Crucifixion faced the west and a 'doom picture', or representation of the Day of Judgment, faced the east. The canopies of the screen and its loft were decorated with gold stars. Tradition avers that when Cromwell's soldiers were lodged there in 1651–1658 they destroyed the tracery work, especially that of the great west window, as well as mutilating the statues and carvings. Some of their bullets and bullet marks are still visible. The chapter-house remained tolerably entire for a century-and-a-half, being used for Regality Courts; at intervals from 1671 to 1731 the Six Incorporated Trades of Elgin held their meetings in it. On the morning of Easter Sunday 1711 the great central tower fell and thereafter destruction proceeded apace. Thomas Pennant, the English traveller, described the appearance of the building as it was in 1771 thus: 'but that (the tower) in the centre with the spire and whole roofs are fallen in, and form most aweful fragments, mixed with the battered monuments of knights and prelates'. For well-nigh a century the ruins were used as a quarry, even the Magistrates in 1800 permitting stones to be taken for the building of their Academy.

In 1807, when the place had become a dump for rubbish, public opinion at last awoke to the scandal, an enclosure wall was built and a keeper appointed. In 1816, and again in 1820, the attention of the Barons of Exchequer (before 1833, the Scottish branch of the Treasury) was directed to the condition of the Cathedral. The ownership of the ruins was by no means clear, but the controversy which had gone on over the Scottish bishoprics and their property for 130 years after the Reformation seemed to have ended with the Crown having a better title than anyone else. The Exchequer acted to preserve one of the western towers, and in 1825 gave a grant towards a keeper's salary. John Shanks was appointed, who 'cleared away with his own hands many thousand cubic yards of rubbish

disclosing the bases of the pillars, collecting the carved fragments and introducing some order and propriety' (as recorded on his tombstone at the south-east corner of the kirkyard): in 1833 he revealed the four steps at the west front doorway. Increasing public interest in the ruins had already been shown in 1826 by the publication of a volume of engravings, with a description. Three of the engravings are reproduced in this guide: on the cover, and as plates 9 and 27 (below). The Crown then initiated works of repair which mark the beginning of the continuous care of the monument, now in the charge of the Secretary of State for Scotland.

Plate 27. The cathedral from the south-east in 1826, from *A series of views . . . of Elgin Cathedral* (1826).

# GLOSSARY

*Abutment:* solid masonry placed to resist and balance the sideways thrust of an arch or vault.

*Aisle:* (in the context of Elgin): part of a church parallel to, and divided by arcades from, the nave, choir or presbytery.

*Alb:* a tunic of white cloth reaching to the feet worn by priests in religious ceremonies.

*Arcade:* a range of arches carried on pillars.

*Aumbry:* a cupboard or wall-recess.

*Bas-relief:* a sculpture in low relief i.e. where the figures etc project only slightly from the background.

*Belfry:* the storey of a tower in which bells are hung.

*Boss:* an ornamental knob or projection at the intersection of ribs in a vault.

*Buttress:* masonry built against or projecting from a wall to give additional strength; or ornamental masonry imitating such a structural device.

*Canon:* a member of the chapter i.e. the body of ecclesiastics associated with a cathedral or religious house.

*Canopy:* a roof-like projection extending over a door, window, tomb, niche etc.

*Cavetto:* a hollow moulding, usually a quarter-circle in section.

*Censer:* a vessel in which incense is burnt.

*Chalice:* the cup used in the celebration of Holy Communion.

*Chanonry:* (Scots): the area containing the dwellings of the Cathedral dignitaries and office-bearers.

*Chapter-house:* the place of assembly for the dean, office-bearers and canons of a cathedral, or the equivalent dignitaries of a monastery, to discuss business.

*Choir:* the area of the church containing the stalls (i.e. seats) of the clergy and choristers who performed the daily round of services.

*Choir-stalls:* wooden seats in the choir, often elaborately carved and provided with wooden canopies.

*Clerestory:* the antique spelling of the word disguises its meaning of a 'clear storey', the upper stage of the main walls of a church above the aisle roofs, pierced by windows which give unobstructed light to the interior.

*Consecration Cross:* a cross usually enclosed within a circle, carved on the walls of a church to mark the dedication of the building to its sacred purpose.

*Cope:* a vestment resembling a cloak made of a semicircular piece of cloth, worn by priests on ceremonial occasions.

*Corbel:* a projecting stone block supporting a member above.

*Crocket:* a decoration in Gothic architecture carved in leaf shapes, regularly spaced on spires, pinnacles, gables, canopies etc.

*Crossing:* the intersection of the main body of a church with its transepts.

*Cusps:* small projecting points in Gothic tracery.

*Diocese:* the district under the spiritual care and jurisdiction of a bishop.

*Dog-tooth:* an ornament consisting of a series of four-pointed stars placed diagonally.

*Elevations:* The vertical faces of a building.

*Engaged shaft:* a pillar or column attached to a wall or architectural feature.

*Enrichment:* the ornament used in the decorative elaboration of a member of a building.

*Eucharist:* the Sacrament of the Lord's Supper or Holy Communion: the consecrated bread and wine.

*Finial:* a formalised flower ornament at the top of a pinnacle, canopy etc.

*Gable:* the triangular upper part of a wall at the end of a roof with sloping sides.

*Gablet:* an ornament shaped like a small gable.

*Guige:* (heraldry): A belt-like support for a shield: a guige being the shoulder belt used for this purpose in warfare.

*Hipped roof:* Having sloping ends instead of vertical gables.

*Incumbency:* the period of tenure of office of an ecclesiastic.

*Jupon:* a sleeveless surcoat worn outside the armour.

*Keystone:* the central topmost stone of an arch.

*Lancet:* a high and narrow opening terminating in a pointed arch.

*Lantern:* part of an upper structure such as a tower, pierced with windows and open below to the main body of a building.

*Lights:* windows or openings to admit light.

*Loft:* a gallery.

*Manse:* an ecclesiastical residence.

*Mitre:* a bishop's tall cap, deeply cleft at the top.

*Mouldings:* the contours or shapes carved in members of a building.

*Muniment:* a document e.g. a title-deed.

*Mural:* within the thickness of a wall.

*Nave:* the part of a church open to the laity.

*Niche:* a recess or hollow in a wall, usually to contain a statue.

*Ogee:* an arch composed of double-curved or S-shaped arcs.

*Parapet:* a low wall at the edge of a roof.

*Parclose Screen:* a partition serving to enclose an altar, chapel etc.

*Pastoral Staff:* part of the insignia of a bishop, representing a shepherd's crook, usually richly ornamented.

*Paten:* the shallow dish on which the bread is laid during the celebration of Holy Communion.

*Pier:* a support of masonry designed to sustain vertical pressure; a pillar from which an arch springs.

*Piscina:* a stone basin for washing the vessels of the Holy Communion.

*Poniard:* a dagger.

*Port:* a gate or gateway; a gatehouse.

*Portal:* a doorway.

*Prebendary:* a canon of a cathedral entitled to a portion of the revenues.

*Precinct:* the ground immediately surrounding a religious house or cathedral, usually marked out by a boundary wall.

*Prelate:* an ecclesiastical dignitary of high rank, especially a bishop.

*Presbytery:* the part of a major church which housed the high altar and the ceremonial area around it.

*Pulpitum:* the screen, of stone or wood, across the west end of the choir.

*Quatrefoil:* an opening or decorative detail having its outline so divided by curvilinear projecting points as to give it the appearance of four leaves or petals.

*Respond:* a half-pillar bonded into a wall and carrying one end of an arch.

*Retable:* a frame enclosing decorated panels above the back of an altar.

*Rood Screen:* a screen across the east end of the nave, on which was raised a painted representation of the Crucifixion (the Anglo-Saxon word *rood* meaning a cross).

*Sacristy:* repository for vestments, etc. in a church.

*Sandstone:* rock of compressed sand, used for fine masonry.

*Sedilia:* stone seats for clergy recessed into the south wall of the presbytery or the chancel.

*Sill:* the lower horizontal part of a window frame.

*Socket Stone:* a stone cut with a recess to secure an upright stone such as the shaft of a cross.

*Spire:* a tall structure rising from a tower and terminating in a point.

*Stall:* a carved seat of wood or stone, usually in a row of similar seats.

*String course:* a narrow horizontal line of projecting masonry carried along a building.

*Tippet:* a band of material worn round the neck of an ecclesiastic with the two ends hanging from the shoulders in front.

*Tracery:* the decorative work in the upper part of a window or panel.

*Transept:* the arms at right angles to the main body of a cross-shaped church.

*Translation:* removal of a bishop to another see.

*Trefoil:* an opening or decorative detail having its outline so divided by curvilinear projecting points as to give it the appearance of a three-lobed leaf.

*Tressure:* (heraldry): a border within the shield; in the Royal Arms of Scotland double with fleurs-de-lys on each side, i.e. in heraldic terms *flory* and *counter-flory*.

*Triforium:* the gallery or arcade in the wall over the arches at the sides of the main body of a large church, being at the level of the aisle roofs.

*Vault:* an arched roof or ceiling of stone.

*Vesica:* an upright almond shape.

*Vestibule:* an antechamber or lobby.

*Wattle:* a panel, partition or fence of interwoven twigs.

*Wyvern:* a dragon-shaped mythical beast.

HMSO  Dd 0287224  9/88  1750  3106/1 (13129)